C000303108

Also available in this series from Quadrille:

the little book of
LUCK

Hardie Grant

QUADRILLE

*"With luck on your side,
you can do without brains."*

GIORDANO BRUNO

Definition of luck

1. a: A force that brings good fortune or adversity.
   b: The events or circumstances that operate for or against an individual.

2. Favouring chance; also: success.

First used in the 15th century, the word 'luck' has its origins in the Middle English word lucke, which comes from the Dutch word luc.

"I am a great believer in luck. The harder I work, the more of it I seem to have."

COLEMAN COX

According to a 2016 survey by 888poker.com, the United Kingdom wins more competitions and sports events per person than anywhere in the world, making it the luckiest place to live.

Top-ten luckiest countries

1. United Kingdom
2. United States
3. Italy
4. France
5. Japan
6. Egypt
7. Germany
8. India
9. Turkey
10. Russia

"If a man's fortune does not fit him, it is like the shoe in the story; if too large it trips him up, if too small it pinches him."

HORACE

What is luck?

An indefinable magical quality that
makes the impossible seem probable,
luck, like a pendulum, swings both
ways. It can lift you up to dance among
the stars or bring you crashing down
just as fast. In a heartbeat, everything
is turned on its head, throwing you
headlong into chance encounters
that will change your world forever.
Heaven-sent opportunities fall at your
feet and all with a roll of the dice.

Seemingly supernatural, luck cannot be captured; it has no physical form but instead manifests as an idea, a concept, a pattern of thought. Most importantly, it is a belief that you are lucky from the top of your head to the tips of your toes – and vice versa.

Remember, wishing good luck to someone in the theatre is bad luck, so say "break a leg" instead.

"*I bear a charméd life.*"

MACBETH TO MACDUFF
In *Macbeth Act V* scene VII
by William Shakespeare

Shakespeare's famous play *Macbeth* is said to be cursed. To avoid bringing bad luck and distaster upon themselves, actors can only refer to the production as 'The Scottish Play' when inside the theatre.

Luck never gives, it only lends.

Everyone is the author of his own good fortune.

FRENCH PROVERB

"When a man's willing and eager, the gods join in."

AESCHYLUS

Some people believe that luck is a gift from the gods. It is not something you're born with; you have no control over it. Instead, you must wait for this magical blessing to be bestowed upon you.

For some, luck can be created out of thin air with logic and application.

For most, it is earned, through the spirit of hard work and applying oneself with a positive attitude.

> "*Fortune knocks at every man's door once in a life, but in a good many cases the man is in a neighboring saloon and does hear her.*"

MARK TWAIN

Luck is an experience, expected or not, that makes you feel on top of the world.

To increase your quota, eliminate all the things that cause you stress. Learn to let go, and instead enjoy the things that make you happy. Positive people attract positive things, so if you want more luck, start with how you feel and what makes you smile.

Luck, like a see-saw, relies on balance. For most it veers from good to bad throughout life. The secret to keeping in the air and on the up is to think 'light', 'positive' and 'hopeful' thoughts. When we do this our spirits are lifted, and we naturally attract good luck.

" You gotta try your luck at least once a day, because you could be going around lucky all day and not even know it."

JIMMY DEAN

According to a UK survey held in 2017, some names are luckier than others. Some 2000 adults were quizzed about how fortunate they felt, and the names they thought were lucky.

Top-ten luckiest ladies' names

1. Kate
2. Sarah
3. Victoria
4. Jane
5. Lucy
6. Mary
7. Elizabeth
8. Emma
9. Julie
10. Sharon

Top 10 luckiest men's names

1. David
2. John
3. Richard
4. Paul
5. Steve
6. James
7. Peter
8. Mark
9. Michael
10. Andrew

You can make your own luck if you have the magic formula.

Positivity + Confidence + Creativity + Spontaneity + Resilience = Luck

"Luck is believing you're lucky."

TENNESSEE WILLIAMS

Self-belief is the foundation from which good luck grows.

Fake it till you make it

Scientists concur that if you believe you're lucky, you will be lucky. Adopting this attitude causes a shift in perspective from a 'woe is me' approach to a more positive outlook, so even when things do go wrong, you'll see the silver lining and be able to move forward. When things go well, you'll be in the right mindset to make the most of opportunities that come your way.

Lucky tip

Every morning and night look in the mirror and repeat this affirmation with confidence: 'I am the luckiest person alive!' Be bold and say it with passion until you start to believe that it is true.

"All of us have bad luck and good luck. The man who persists through the bad luck, who keeps right on going, is the man who is there when the good luck comes and is ready to receive it."

ROBERT COLLIER

Be open in heart and mind

Lucky people say 'yes' to life. They have learned to expect the unexpected. They embrace new challenges and go with the flow, rather than trying to control every single event.

Lucky tip

Welcome each day in a positive way. Throw back the curtains, stand feet hip-width apart and open your arms wide, as if drawing in the view. Reach up to the ceiling, as far as you can go and feel the gentle stretch along your spine. Slowly bring your arms down and curl forwards, letting them hang to the floor, then unfurl and return to a standing position. A flexible body means a flexible mind.

Trust your intuition

Research shows that lucky people are tuned in to their sixth sense. They trust their instincts and know whether something feels right or wrong.

Lucky tip

When sizing up a situation, take a moment to breathe. Place your hands on your stomach and take long, deep breaths. Focus on the rise and fall of your chest. Relax and notice any feelings or impressions that arise.

"Luck affects everything. Let your hook always be cast in the stream. When you least expect it, there will be fish."

OVID

See what you want to be

Those with luck on their side tend to picture what they want and ultimately have faith that they will reach their goal. This self-belief, along with the creative power of the mind, goes some way to explaining their success.

Lucky tip

Imagine where you'd like to be in a year's time. What would make you feel like the luckiest person on the earth? Picture the situation you'll be in and what you'll be doing. See yourself thriving. How will you feel at this time? Conjure up these emotions and enjoy them, as if it were happening now. Repeat daily, and over time you should notice a change in the way you feel and behave, while also experiencing your fair share of good luck.

"Luck is tenacity of purpose."

ELBERT HUBBARD

"Luck is the sense to recognise an opportunity and the ability to take advantage of it."

SAMUEL GOLDWYN

Take a risk

Lucky people are bold. They don't sit on the sidelines saying 'what if?' when presented with an opportunity. They seize the day. Sometimes they fail, in which case they dust themselves down, consider any lessons learned and move forwards. Mostly they succeed. Whatever happens, their go-getting attitude means they always win in some way.

Lucky tip

Step outside your comfort zone by trying something new, whether that's a different coffee place or an alternative route to work. Even small steps that place you in unfamiliar territory are enough to boost self-confidence and spontaneity.

Appreciate what you have

Those who have luck on their side are always grateful. Rather than focusing on what they don't have, they are thankful for their blessings – even the small ones.

Lucky tip

Cultivate gratitude by giving thanks every evening before bed for all the things that you have, all the things that went well, and all the people who have helped to make your day better.

If at first you don't succeed,
try, try, try again!

"Luck is not chance—
It's Toil.
Fortune's expensive smile
is earned—"

EMILY DICKINSON

Some psychologists believe that a person's luck potential, also known as the 'success quotient', is established by the age of 10. If a child has warm and loving parents who are open with their emotions, and if one or both are successful in their field of choice, then their success quotient will be high. Chances are, they'll be subject to a substantial amount of good luck when they reach adulthood.

"One half of life is luck; the other half is discipline – and that's the important half, for without discipline you wouldn't know what to do with your luck."

CARL ZUCKMEYER,

The Hawaiian word for luck is *kūlia*, but this has a dual meaning and is also interpreted as strife or strive. Simply put, the more challenges you face, the more likely you are to attract luck.

Pono, is another Hawaiian word meaning luck. In this case it refers to a general feeling of well-being, prosperity and good fortune, but the underlying theme is being or doing good for others. The Hawaiians believe that doing nice things for others brings more good fortune to your door. In essence, be kind and treat others how you'd like to be treated and you'll get Lady Luck on your side

"Fortune always will confer an aura of worth, unworthily, and in this world the lucky person passes for a genius."

EURIPIDES

Wish good luck around the world!

Bonne chance!

Viel Glück!

¡Buena suerte!

In bocca al lupo!

Lycka till!

Laki maika'i!

Zhù nǐ hǎo yùn!

Haeng-un-eul bibnida!

Ádh mór!

Boa sorte!

"Fortune is the rod of the weak and the staff of the brave."

JAMES RUSSELL LOWELL

Lady luck

Known by many different guises, Lady Luck was first recognised as the Greek goddess Tyche, whose name translated means 'luck', or 'chance'. Her Roman counterpart was Fortuna, and both deities were associated with good luck and abundance. From the fifth century, the poet Pindar refers to Tyche as a 'saviour goddess', a nod to the life-changing fortune she brings.

Often pictured with the wheel of fate in her hands or holding an overflowing cornucopia to indicate prosperity and wealth, Tyche was a popular deity and her image adorned wash houses, temples, coins and jewellery. The ancients petitioned her for help and built shrines and altars to win her favour.

"Fortune has something of the nature of a woman. If she is too intensely wooed, she commonly goes the further away."

CHARLES V

Spin the wheel

Coins are flipped, dice tossed and the roulette wheel spins in a bid to get fortune's attention. The common denominator is the circular movement: everything turns continuously like Lady Luck's wheel of fate and the cycles of life. For those wishing for divine intervention, a simple ritual that combines the spinning of a wheel with positive thought may be enough to transform luck and was certainly put to use by the superstitious ancients.

Lucky tip

If you can't find a wheel or coin to spin, picture yourself on a giant Ferris wheel. Feel the carriage lift off the ground, taking you high into the air. As you do this, make a wish for success. Good luck!

" To attract good fortune, spend a new penny on an old friend, share an old pleasure with a new friend and lift up the heart of a true friend by writing his name on the wings of a dragon."

ANONYMOUS

Luck and superstition go hand in hand. If you believe in the existence of one, you'll most likely believe in the other. Those who are lucky and not superstitious tend to think of their luck in more practical terms, being both earned and deserved, rather than as a supernatural gift.

Rabbit rabbit

During the 1900s a strange
superstition emerged in the UK,
and while the reasoning behind this
is unclear, it's still practised today.
On the first day of a new month it is
tradition to say 'Rabbit,' or 'Rabbit,
rabbit,' or even 'White rabbits' to
ensure good luck for the weeks that
follow. Should you forget to chant
the bunny first thing, you can still
secure your share of fortune by saying
'Black rabbit,' or 'Tibbar, tibbar,'
which is rabbit backwards, before
you go to bed.

Touch wood

Knocking on wood is a popular Western superstition, which dates back to pre-Christian times when trees were considered sacred by the Celts and Druids. Inhabited by spirits known as dryads, it was common practice for the ancients to knock against the trunk, and then speak their deepest wishes and dreams in the hope that the dryads would make them come true. Today the phrase 'touch wood' is often used to avoid tempting fate, or to secure good fortune.

Blarney luck

The legendary Blarney Stone of Ireland was originally thought to be something called Jacob's Pillow, brought to Ireland by the prophet Jeremiah. While some stories claim it was brought back to Blarney Castle from the Crusades and is really the 'stone Ezel' behind which David hid on Jonathan's advice when he fled from his enemy, Saul. Set in the wall below the battlements, visitors come from miles around to dangle precariously by the ankles and give it a kiss, an act that bestows luck and the gift of eloquence on the kisser.

"Superstition is the poetry of life."

JOHANN WOLFGANG VON GOETHE

"Henceforth I ask not good fortune. I myself am good fortune."

WALT WHITMAN

Lucky superstitions from around the world...

In Thailand, men choose to wear a penis amulet made from wood or bone around their necks. Known as a *palad khik*, it's thought to bring enormous amounts of good luck to the wearer.

Be careful never to cut the branches of an elder tree because, in Latvia and Lithuania, dwarves lived beneath the roots. If allowed to live unharmed, the dwarves would bring luck to the area.

The Chinese always keep their front door, porch and entrance clean and clear of clutter to ensure a steady flow of good luck into their home. If this area becomes untidy or dirty, then fortune is likely to go elsewhere!

In Serbia, it's common practice to throw water behind a person as a way of wishing them good luck. This is often carried out before interviews, tests and big events to ensure success.

If you happen to step in dog poo while in France, take a note of which foot is sullied. If it's your left foot, then you'll soon be blessed with good luck; if it's your right, then bad luck is on its way.

Breaking bottles of alcohol is the Japanese way to get the attention of the universe. It's thought that smashing the bottles will attract good luck and wealth, depending on how expensive the contents are!

The Sensoji Temple in East Tokyo is a good-luck hotspot because of its giant incense burner. Visitors spend hours standing in this 'smoke bath,' wafting the vapours around their bodies to attract luck and health.

In Argentina, it's a custom to eat beans on New Year's Eve or New Year's Day. This tasty staple not only provides sustenance but ensures luck and job security for the year ahead.

Newlyweds that hail from the Netherlands often plant pine trees outside their homes. This practice is thought to bring good fortune and fertility. Trees are considered lucky and are often incorporated into the marriage ceremony as a way of blessing the couple.

The hollow women of Sweden

Beware the *Skogsra*, the wild forest
spirit of Sweden. In return for bringing
luck to hunters (by blowing on their
gun), the *Skogsra* then demands to be
made love to. The hunters generally
oblige, only to discover her back is like
the hollow of a tree, whereupon they
flee into the night.

Good luck grapes in Peru

On the stroke of midnight Peruvians dive under the table and eat 12 grapes as quickly as possible to guarantee good luck for the forthcoming year – one grape for each month. Just be careful not to choke!

Russian good luck house fairy

Living behind the stove or under the hearth are *Domovoy*, the chief house spirit of Russian folklore. The *Domovoy* should be greeted as "Grandfather" and, if he is adequately provided with food and drink, will bring luck to the household

Bad luck in Portugal

The Portuguese word for bad luck is *azar* and tradition says that when you have a run of it, you must immediately visit a witch to usher in a spell of good luck instead.

Lucky proverbs

"The day you decide to do it is your lucky day."

JAPANESE PROVERB

"When luck enters, give him a seat!"

JEWISH PROVERB

Lucky proverbs

*"Fortune and misfortune are
two buckets in the same well."*

HENRY WARD BEECHER

*"Luck will carry a man across the
brook if he is not too lazy to leap."*

DANISH PROVERB

Lucky proverbs

"No one is luckier than he who believes in his luck."

GERMAN PROVERB

"Luck sometimes visits a fool but it never sits down with him."

GERMAN PROVERB

Lucky proverbs

"*With money in your pocket,
you are wise and you are
handsome and you sing well too.*"

YIDDISH PROVERB

"*Better an ounce of luck
than a pound of gold.*"

YIDDISH PROVERB

"Find a penny, pick it up and all day long you'll have good luck" *

* Some say the penny should only be picked up if lying heads up.

The key to living well is to say no to cynicism. All those reading this and scoffing at the idea a penny will usher in good luck, think again. Little charms and lucky pennies obviously don't in themselves summon good luck, but the feelings they engender do. So be light-hearted, pick up that penny, let it put a spring in your step and bring a bounce to your day. If you *think* finding a penny and picking it up will bring you good luck, it *will*.

Lucky / unlucky coins

Buddy Holly sadly died in a plane crash in Iowa in 1959 – the day the music died. Fellow musicians Ritchie Valens and Tommy Allsup tossed a coin to see who would fly with Buddy. The coin flip was lucky for Tommy Allsup and fatally unlucky for Ritchie Valens – he of "La Bamba" fame.

While it does seem to be complete luck whether a coin lands on heads or tails, the ancients used to believe that the chance outcome was actually the manifestation of divine will.

"Live as brave men; and if fortune is adverse, front its blows with brave hearts"

CICERO

How to defeat bad luck the Ancient Greek way:

1. Look bad luck in the eye.
   Know your enemy.

2. Fight it. Don't hide because
   bad luck will always find you.

3. Be brave – fight your bad luck
   with a brave heart.

Dolphins are considered lucky by many ancient cultures, including Greece, Sumer, Egypt, and Rome. The belief stems from the fact that sailors, who spent several months or years away at sea, would know land was near when they saw dolphins swimming around their ships.

The Ancient Romans so revered luck (or fortune) that in c. AD 106 the Emperor Trajan put up a temple to the Goddess Fortuna, the omnipotent power of the universe.

*" There are good and bad times,
but our mood changes more often
than our fortune"*

THOMAS CARLYLE

An old story tells of the rich man whose wife did not love him. One day, he gave away his fortune and his wife saw her husband blossom from a rich but mean man, to a poor yet gentle soul. They left their house for a small cottage and found happiness, dying years later in each other's arms. Villagers thought great misfortune had befallen the couple, yet all that had changed was the man's mood. He decided to seek happiness and love rather than riches and greed. How we approach luck, whether good or bad, affects all aspects of our lives, from material prosperity to emotional wellbeing.

"Fortune favours the prepared mind"

LOUIS PASTEUR

The Scout's Motto, coined by founder Robert Baden-Powell is 'Be Prepared'. He wrote in *Scouting for Boys* in 1907, *"Be prepared in mind...by having thought out beforehand any accident or situation that might occur, so that you know the right thing to do at the right moment, and are willing to do it."*

Whether arranging a small journey or an exhilarating adventure, preparing and planning are vital in reducing the chance of pesky bad luck blighting your travels.

"A heart well prepared for adversity in bad times hopes and in good times fears for a change in fortune"

HORACE

Jinx: dictionary definition:

noun

1. Person or thing that brings bad luck
2. Bring bad luck to, cast an evil spell on

"Friends and acquaintances are the surest passport to fortune"

ARTHUR SCHOPENHAUER

Good friends = good luck.
Bad friends = bad luck

Bad King John was King of England
from 1199 – 1216. His reign was beset
with personal and kingdom-wide
disasters. He imprisoned his first wife
and murdered his nephew. Not only
did Bad King John lose the territories
England controlled in Normandy
but he also lost the Royal Treasury
in a tidal estuary. All of this would
have come as no surprise to the
medieval chronicler who noticed that,
as a young Prince, John surrounded
himself with friends who "sniggered"
when courtiers tripped over.
Bad friends made a bad king.

*"Everyone is the builder
of their own luck"*

ANONYMOUS

Three ways to build good luck

1. Expect good things to happen

2. Do good and good will come to you

3. Plan for what you want to do

"Diligence is the mother of good fortune"

BENJAMIN DISRAELI

"*Fortune truly helps those who are of good judgement*"

EURIPIDES

"A woman who can create her own job is the woman who will win fame and fortune"

AMELIA EARHART

Freedom for luck

Freedom walks hand in hand with good luck. Good luck will not fall on those who are not at liberty to make their own decisions, run their own lives, nor master their fate.

First find your freedom, whether it is emotional, financial or spiritual. Secondly embrace your freedom and good luck will join you on your journey.

"You luck is not something to discover, but something to seek and unpack within yourself"

ANONYMOUS

Don't worry if a bird defecates on you –
it's good luck! This rather dubious spot
of luck comes from the idea that your
suffering will eventually be rewarded.

Synonyms for luck...

Advantage
Chance
Destiny
Fate
Felicity
Fluke
Fortune
Karma
Kismet
Lot
Prosperity
Success

"Fortune makes a fool of those she favours too much"

HORACE

"*Good luck will reveal the door
but you have to open it yourself*"

ANONYMOUS

The eight Tibetan symbols of good luck:

The Endless or Eternal Knot
The Lotus Flower
The Treasure Vase
The White Conch Shell
The Pair of Golden Fishes
The Parasol (or Umbrella)
The Victory Banner
The Golden Wheel or Dharma Wheel

"I know he's a good general, but is he lucky?"

"Look, sometimes, no matter how hard you try, you need a bit of luck."

BEAR GRYLLS

Girls' names that mean 'luck':

Amber
Lucky
Shreya
Fayola
Felicity
Kiaria
Seven
Serendipity
Zada
Sapphire

Boys' names that mean 'luck':

Asher
Edmund
Felix
Madoc
Lucky
Quin
Chance
Fortune
Parvais
Said

Four leaf clovers

Four leaf clovers are traditionally supposed to bring good luck to the finder. According to some folk traditions each leaf has a different meaning: the first stands for hope, the second, faith, the third, love and the fourth brings money. So keep your eyes peeled next time you're idling on a lawn on a warm summer's day.

Lucky number seven

Seven oceans, the Jewish seven blessings at a weddings, seven colours in the rainbow, the Christian idea of seven virtues, seven days of the week, seven continents, the Islamic seven number of heavens...there are certainly more than seven reasons why the number seven is supposed to be lucky. Across all cultures and religions, the number seven seems to have a special lucky significance. Whether it's because God made the world in six days and rested on the seventh, or that Snow White had seven dwarfs, there is just something about that number.

Seven ways to wish someone good luck

1. Good luck!
2. Break a leg!
3. Knock 'em dead!
4. Blow them away!
5. Best of luck!
6. You'll do great!
7. Fingers crossed!

Three Chinese lucky colours

Red: happiness, success and fortune
Yellow: representing the earth, yellow is the colour and royalty
Green: wealth and purity

A report for the Edinburgh Science Festival suggested a link between birth month and perceived good luck. May was found to be the luckiest month, with October the unluckiest

Choosing lucky numbers

There is downside to choosing lucky numbers for lottery tickets – other people will too. On November 14, 1995, the winning UK lottery numbers were 7, 17, 23, 32, 38, 42 and 48, of which many are lucky numbers. 133 tickets shared the £16 million prize with each winner receiving just £120,000 – not so lucky after all.

People who consider themselves to be lucky are:

1. Skilled at noticing opportunities

2. Listen to their initiative

3. Maintain positive expectations

Lucky prime numbers

Mathematicians are not immune to the idea of lucky numbers. In number theory, employing a special mathematical sieve generates 'lucky numbers'. The 'lucky numbers' that include prime numbers are known as 'lucky primes'.

Lucky prime numbers:

3, 7, 13, 31, 37, 43, 67, 73, 79, 127, 151, 163, 193, 211, 223, 241, 283, 307, 331, 349, 367, 409, 421, 433, 463, 487, 541, 577, 601, 613... the list of lucky prime numbers can go on to infinity.

How to find your lucky life path number:

Write out your date of birth.

14th December 2001

Month: 12 = 1+2 = 3

Day: 14 = 1+4 = 5

Year: 2001 = 2+1 = 3

Add master number.

3+5+3 = 11

1+1 = 2

Life path number is 2

Chinese lucky numbers: 6, 8, 9

Number 6: life going smoothly.
Number 8: wealth and fortune.
Number 9: everlasting longevity and good fortune.

Chinese unlucky numbers: 4, 7

Number 4: death.
Number 7: the idea of something being gone, or a cheat.

Fortune cookies

Who doesn't love a fortune cookie? The small crispy shell opens to reveal a positive aphorism or prophesy, contained within. Over three billion are made and enjoyed each year around the world. Here are three fortune cookie sayings:

"Nothing is impossible to a willing heart."

"Don't pursue happiness, create it."

"He who throws mud loses ground."

Good luck dragon of Mons

Visit Mons in Belgium on Trinity Sunday and you might witness the parade of a dragon with an escort of wild men, clowns and hobbyhorses. While the dragon attacks with its tail, onlookers try to pluck off its hairs and ribbons for good luck.

Dancing for good luck

As early as the 16th century in Southern Romania, groups of fraternal dancers called the Căluşari danced to bring good luck. The groups of seven men would meet on Whit Sunday, don white dresses and dance their way from village to village. Their athletic and acrobatic dancing, combined with their elegant outfits and jingling spurs, brought good luck and good health to all houses they visited.

When next baking hot cross buns for Easter, don't forget to hang one somewhere in the house to ensure good luck for the rest of the year.

Be like the Estonians and bring good luck to the forthcoming harvest by having a bonfire on midsummer's eve and...then jumping over it.

Linking a chicken or turkey's wishbone with your pinkie finger and pulling with a partner until it snaps, is a good luck ritual. Thought to have begun with the Ancient Etruscans who believed birds foretold the future, the tradition travelled via Ancient Rome to England and then with the Pilgrim Fathers to America. The person who snaps the wishbone and wins the largest half will have good luck.

Whether wide spread in the United States, or not, there are tales of Americans, who on receiving their first Christmas card of the year post a dollar bill to the sender. This charming custom is said to ensure the receiver has good luck for the coming year.

Prince Albert brought lots of brilliant German Christmas traditions with him when he married Queen Victoria of England. One of the best is the coin in the Christmas pudding.

When each member of the family stirred the Christmas pudding mixture six weeks before Christmas, a silver sixpence would be dropped in. Whoever found the coin in their slice of pudding on Christmas Day could claim good luck for the year ahead (so long as they didn't crack their tooth on discovery).

Lucky foods to eat at New Year

1. Ring shaped breads – to represent the year coming full circle.

2. Pork – pigs are lovely and fat and therefore symbolize prosperity.

3. Lentils – their round shape suggests money. The Italians enjoy *Cotechino con Lenticchie* on New Year's Day, a delicious combination of pork sausages and lentils for double good luck.

4. *Vasilopita* is eaten on New Year's Day in Greece and parts of the Balkans. It's a gorgeous cake where a coin is hidden and brings good luck to the person who receives it.

Scottish custom suggests the practice of 'first footing' at New Year. To invite good luck for the coming year, Scots insist a dark-haired male should be the first into the house and he should carry bread, salt, coal or a drink representing food, flavour, financial prosperity and good cheer.

In Wales, it's tradition at New Year to open the back door to let bad luck out and the front door to let good luck in.

If you're in Wales in spring, try to find the first daffodil of the season – it will bring you good luck!

"Something old, something new, something borrowed something blue… and a silver sixpence in her shoe"

Famously, to guarantee good luck for the wedding and marriage, brides have to wear something old, something new, something borrowed, something blue, but less well known is that the rhyme ends with "and a silver sixpence in her shoe." Just before he walked her down the aisle, the father of the bride would slip a silver sixpence in his daughter's shoe to show he wished prosperity for her marriage.

If a bride finds a spider in her wedding dress, no need to fear, it's a sign of good luck. This dates back to the idea that Mary, Joseph and the baby Jesus hid in a cave from Herod's soldiers. A spider spun a web over the entrance to protect them, and for evermore became a symbol of good luck.

In Bulgaria the bride is advised to step into the church right foot first in order to have a lucky marriage.

Many American families have a perculiar family heirloom, whereby a tiny mustard seed is implanted into a necklace. This is worn by female members of the family when marrying, to bring good luck. Originally the mustard seed was a sign of faith but has now become a secular symbol of good luck.

Brides and grooms in Thailand ask their guest to tie a white string around each of their wrists. To give the couple maximum luck, guests need to wear them for three days.

Chimney sweep

We have King George II of England to thank for the idea that chimney sweeps are good luck. The story goes that the king's life was saved by a chimney sweep who stopped his horse after it had bolted. The King then decreed that chimney sweeps should be seen as lucky.

The legend has grown to make it particularly auspicious for a bride to see a chimney sweep on her wedding day... so long as he doesn't get her dress dirty. If he should happen to kiss the bride, then she is truly blessed, while the groom must seek a hearty handshake for his share of good fortune.

Black cats – lucky or unlucky?

Owing to their colouring and nocturnal habits, black cats are deemed to have something of the night about them. Associations with witches have not helped their cause. Whether they are unlucky or lucky, depends entirely on where you live.

"A black cat crossing your path signifies it is going somewhere."

GROUCHO MARX

Lucky black cats

Scotland – if a black cat enters a house it will bring prosperity.

England – it's a good omen if a black cat crosses your path.

Ancient Egypt – the goddess Bastet was depicted as a black cat.

Japan – if you see a black cat crossing your path, you say *konichiwa* and seize the good luck.

Italy – if you hear a black cat sneeze, you are in for a streak of good luck.

Russia – all cats are considered lucky in Russia!

Unlucky black cats

America – The Pilgrim Fathers thought black cats were part demon.

Germany (and most of Europe) – if a cat crosses your path from left to right it is a bad omen.

China – black cats are believed to be harbingers of famine and poverty.

Ukraine – people will change direction to avoid walking where a black cat has walked.

King Charles I of England had a treasured pet black cat. Legend tells that on its death, the king lamented that his luck had gone. The very next day, he was arrested and charged with treason...and later executed in 1649.

The Maneki Neko is the name for Japan's lucky cat figurine. Coming in many colours, the cat is easily recognisable as it is always holding up one beckoning paw. The Maneki Neko is thought to bring good fortune and wealth to its owner.

In the United Kingdom, if you see a fallen eyelash on someone's cheek, pick it off and present it to the owner, who will then blow it away while wishing for good luck.

Cornish school girls however, say that a loose eyelash must be placed on the tip of the nose or the back of the hand. If it is successfully blown off, the accompanying wish will materialize.

In America it is perfectly acceptable to reach forward and un-swivel a necklace whose clasp is lying the wrong way. You then say to the necklace's wearer, "make a wish". Good luck is said to come to both.

Finding a red and black spotted ladybird cheers anyone's day. It's also said to bring good luck and free you of the day's problems. If a ladybird lands on you when you are ill and then alights, it will take your illness away with it.

The scarab beetle is sacred to Ancient Egypt and has been a sign of good luck for thousands of years. The thinking goes, that because they were so protective of their eggs, they would be protective too of human hearts.

Lucky animals:

Cranes
Dolphins
Eagles
Elephants
Falcons
Frogs
Pigs
Red bats
Tortoises
Turtles
Tigers

Amber, that deep golden resin, is thought by some to be part of the sun and contains within it the power to bring good fortune. When rubbed, it sometimes gives off sparks, which is why it is considered a lucky charm.

Sapphires, those inky blue gems, have been revered as lucky jewels since ancient times. The Ancient Greeks believed that wearing sapphires invited the favour of the gods.

Need luck in getting pregnant? A man wearing a rabbit's foot around his neck will soon father a child, and a woman doing the same will soon carry one.

Though some claim that it was the Ancient Celts who first believed a rabbit's foot to be lucky, it seems it was actually 19th century Americans. Sales of lucky rabbit feet began in earnest in 1880s New Orleans after the adoption from West African folklore. But do make sure it's a right foot, as the left foot is cursed...

Before we received our dopamine buzz from social media likes, moments of coincidental thrill would be shared and were said to mean good luck. In America, if you are hanging out with friends and all notice that the time is 11.11am or 11.11pm, it's a lucky moment and everyone has to make a wish.

"What we wish, we readily believe, and what we ourselves think, we imagine others think also."

JULIUS CAESAR

Salute the magpie

In Britain it is common practice on seeing a magpie to say "Good morning Mr Magpie" to ensure good luck for the day ahead.

To be extra sure of good luck, you say, "Good morning Mr Magpie. How's your wife today?" Seeing a solitary bird is considered to be unlucky – by pretending there is another bird nearby you keep this bad luck at bay.

Counting magpies

"*One for sorrow, two for joy, three for a girl, four for a boy, five for silver, six for gold and seven for a secret never to be told.*"

Hang a Native American dream catcher above a baby's cradle to ensure good dreams. Dream catchers are one of the most popular good luck charms in northern America.

Lucky symbols in dreams

Encountering a bear in your dreams is said to bring good luck.

Seeing a chicken with hatching eggs means your dreams will materialise.

A coffin appearing in your dreams is always a symbol of good luck.

The presence of water is sign that financial success is imminent.

Luck of the Irish

The Irish have have always been seen as lucky and there are many Irish lucky charms should you wish to borrow some of their good fortune.

Leprechauns: catch one of these small bearded men and he will lead you to the pot of gold at the end of the rainbow in return for his freedom.

The Irish Harp: said to be the only instrument played during the crusades of the 12th century, the Irish harp is a symbol of freedom.

Claddaugh Rings: depicting two hands holding a heart, these rings will keep you lucky in love.

"If you're lucky enough to be Irish you're lucky enough."

ANONYMOUS

Don't worry if you spill tea leaves in the house – it's good luck.

Paint your front door red to bring good luck into your home.

Good luck cauls

To be born "with the caul", where a baby is delivered with a piece of birth membrane remaining on its head, is said to bring a lifetime of good luck and protection from drowning. Historically, cauls were kept as a precious talisman. Sailors paid highly to buy a preserved caul before embarking on a long voyage.

Famous people born "with the caul":

Charlemagne
Lord Byron
Sigmund Freud
Napoleon

The lucky bird

Sailors set great store by maritime symbols with the sighting of the majestic albatross being a particularly auspicious event. In Coleridge's epic poem, *The Rime of the Ancient Mariner*, when the narrator killed an albatross the sailors made him wear the dead bird around his neck.

*"Ah! well a-day! what evil looks
Had I from old and young!
Instead of the cross, the Albatross
About my neck was hung."*

COLERIDGE

Good luck at sea

Superstitious sailors have many ways to attract good luck to their vessels.

Black cats: having a black cat aboard a ship is a sign of a safe voyage thanks to their apparent ability to fend off storms.

Cormorants: seeing one of these birds was believed by Norwegian sailors to be a good omen.

Tattoos: By having a tattoo of a pig or hen, sailors believed they would be rescued if shipwrecked.

Lucky horseshoe

One of the most famous good luck symbols is the horseshoe. To discover an old horseshoe, particularly with the nails still attached, is said to bestow the finder with protection and good fortune.

The luck of the horseshoe is thanks to St. Dunstan who apparently trapped the devil and made him promise not to enter the house of a Christian – who would be made recognisable by the horseshoe hanging over his door.

How to hang a lucky horseshoe?

Debate rages in the homes of the lucky over whether to hang the horseshoe upside down or not.

Pointing upwards: good luck is held within the horseshoe and is kept safely to protect the house.

Pointing downwards: good luck pours down on everyone who walks beneath the horseshoe into the house.

"I have seen a horse-shoe nailed on a cottage threshold as a preservative against a witch – the idea being that she could not step over cold iron."

EDWARD MOOR

"Fortune sides with him who dares."

VIRGIL

BIBLIOGRAPHY & FURTHER READING:

Books

Bechtel, Stefan, *The Good Luck Book* (Workman Publishing, 1997)

Cocker, Mark, *Crow Country* (Vintage, 2016)

Collier, Robert, *Secret of the Ages* (Sublime Books, 1926)

Dickinson, Emily, *The Complete Poems* (Faber & Faber, 2016)

Gimson, Andrew, *Gimson's Kings & Queens* (Square Peg, 2015)

Jones, Peter, *Veni Vidi Vici* (Atlantic Books, 2014)

Kaplan, Janice, *How Luck Happens* (Penguin Random House, 2018)

Knowles, Elizabeth, *The Oxford Dictionary of Quotations* (Oxford University Press, 2009)

Rhodes, Chloe, *Black Cats and Evil Eyes* (Michael O'Mara, 2015)

Robert, Frank, *Success and Luck: Good Fortune and the Myth of Meritocracy* (Princeton University Press, 2016)

Roud, Steve, *The Penguin Guide to the Superstitions of Britain and Ireland* (Penguin, 2006)

Roud, Steve and Simpson, Jacqueline, *The Oxford Dictionary of English Folklore* (Oxford University Press, 2003)

Simpson, Jacqueline, *European Mythology* (Hamlyn, 1988)

Simpson, Jacqueline and Westwood, Jennifer, *The Lore of the Land* (Penguin Books, 2006)

Struthers, Jane, *Red Sky at Night* (Ebury Press, 2009)

Weinstein, Ellen, *Recipes for Good Luck* (Chronicle Books, 2018)

Whitman, Walt, *The Complete Poems of Walt Whitman* (Wordsworth Poetry Library, 1995)

Williams, Tennessee, *A Street Car Named Desire* (Penguin Modern Classics, 2009)

Wiseman, Richard, *The Little Book of Luck* (Arrow, 2004)

Websites

makemelucky.com

Documentary

Derren Brown: The Experiements, The Secret of Luck (2011)

QUOTES ARE TAKEN FROM:

Aeschylus was an ancient Greek tragedian.

Amelia Earhart was an American aviation pioneer.

Arthur Schopenhauer was a 19th century German philosopher.

Bear Grylls is an English explorer, adventurer and Chief Scout.

Benjamin Disraeli was a Victorian British Prime Minister.

Boethius was a Roman philosopher of the 6th century.

Carl Zuckmeyer was a German writer and playwright.

Charles V was ruler of the Holy Roman Empire, the Spanish Empire and was the Duchy of Burgundy during the 16th century.

Cicero was a Roman orator and statesman.

Coleman Cox was an early 20th century creator of bon mots.

Edward Moor was an English antiquarian.

Elbert Hubbard was an American idealist, writer and editor.

Emily Dickinson was an American poet.

Euripides was a tragedian of classic Athens.

Giordano Bruno was a 16th century Italian Dominican friar.

Groucho Marx was an American comedian.

Henry Ward Beecher was a social reformer.

Horace was an Ancient Roman lyric poet.

James Russell Lowell was an American poet, editor and diplomat.

Jimmy Dean was a country and western singer.

Johann Wolfgang von Goethe was a German writer and statesman.

Addison founded *The Spectator* magazine.

Caesar was a politician and general of the late Roman republic ultimately seized power of the Roman Empire.

Pasteur was a French chemist.

Mark Twain was an American writer, author of *Tom Sawyer*.

Napoleon Bonaparte was a French statesman and military leader who came to prominence during the French Revolution.

Ovid was a Roman poet.

Robert Baden Powell was British Army officer who later founded The Boy Scouts Association and Girl Guides.

Robert Collier was a self-help author.

Samuel Goldwyn was a Polish-American film producer.

Samuel Taylor Coleridge was an English poet and literary critic who founded the Romantic Movement along with William Wordsworth.

Tennessee Williams was an American playwright.

Thomas Carlyle was a 19th century historian.

Virgil was an ancient Roman poet.

Walt Whitman was an American poet, essayist and journalist.

William Shakespeare was English playwright, poet and literary giant.

Publishing Director Sarah Lavelle
Editor Harriet Butt
Assistant Editor Harriet Webster
Words Alison Davies, Joanna Gray
Series Designer Emily Lapworth
Designer Monika Adamczyk
Production Director Vincent Smith
Production Controller Sinead Hering

Published in 2019 by Quadrille,
an imprint of Hardie Grant Publishing

Quadrille
52-54 Southwark Street
London SE1 1UN
quadrille.com

Cataloguing in Publication Data: a
catalogue record for this book is available
from the British Library.

ISBN 978 1 78713 379 2

Printed in China